A Humble Spirit

Creative Writing For Christian Teens

New Testament

Cheryl Pryor

Arlington & Amelia

Arlington & Amelia Publishing

ArlingtonAmeliaPub@cfl.rr.com

ISBN:1-886541-41-8
ISBN:13-978-1-886541-41-2

TABLE OF CONTENTS

HOW TO USE THIS BOOK

'A Humble Spirit' is an introduction to creative writing for Christian teens focusing on scriptures and living a Godly lifestyle.

'A Humble Spirit' is meant to encourage, uplift, and inspire teens to fill their lives with love, joy, faith, and good works.

This book can be used as a teen Bible study, part of a homeschool requirement for a high school ½ credit, or for the purpose of edifying your teen and encouraging them to grow spiritually.

'A Humble Spirit' part 2 in the series of Christian Writing for Teens Series focuses on the New Testament and can be used on it's own or in addition to 'With Wings Like Eagles' part 1 of the series which focuses on the Old Testament.

If you are homeschooling, you may wish to use this course for a high school ½ credit towards an English/Creative Writing credit or for Bible. If you are planning on using this book for a high school credit, check with your state or local homeschooling group to see how this can be used for your child's curriculum.

The book can be used in the order it is written, completing one chapter before going on to the next or each day use an assignment from a different chapter. It is entirely up to you.

Other Books by Cheryl Pryor

A Humble Spirit: New Testament Creative Writing For Christian Teens

With Wings Like Eagles: Old Testament Creative Writing For Christian Teens

The Big Book of Old Testament Bible Trivia

The Big Book of New Testament Bible Trivia

Living The Word of God

Women In History Trivia

Where In The U.S. Am I?

Where In The World Am I?

The Big Book of Presidential Trivia

The Big Book of First Ladies Trivia

Presidents, First Ladies, & First Family Trivia

Presidents Trivia Challenge

First Family Trivia

Children Of The Presidents

American Revolution & The Birth of A Nation Trivia

Chosen

Pregnancy Journal

Precious Moments

Treasured Moments of My Child

My Mother's Life Story

My Father's Life Story

How Much Do You *Really* Know About The Love Of Your Life?

Couples Game Night Challenge

RV Travel & Expense Journal

Wedding Survival Guide

Write Now

Legacy

Children's Books

My Child's Keepsake Journal

Trivia For Kids: The Presidents

Trivia For Kids: First Ladies

From the series: The Sullivan Family Series

Savannah In The Big Move

Savannah On Stage

Savannah On Horseback

Savannah in Look What Followed Me Home

Savannah & The Grumpy Neighbor

Savannah & The Mad Scientist

From the series: Savannah's World Travels Series

Savannah's Disney World Celebration

Savannah Goes To Paris

1

Finding Comfort In Scriptures :
Topics You Will Face In Life

In this section a verse from the New Testament will be given.

Write how the scripture applies to your life and what it means to you

1) Peer pressure can be tough. You want to be accepted, though you know what your peers want you to do goes against everything you have been taught and believe in.

It takes strength of character to stand up for what you know is the right thing to do. Even Jesus was tempted, as you too, will be.

There may be times you will be laughed at or even lose *"friends"* over your stance. Your actions may convict others and make them ponder on your actions. Some may admire you though may not be strong enough to admit it in front of others. At the same time, others may ridicule you. You may have some take your side with you, but even if not; you as a Christian know what you should do.

Matthew 4:1- Then Jesus was led up by the Spirit into the wilderness to be tempted by the devil.

How can you plan ahead so when these circumstances come up you are prepared to stand firm in your faith?

_____

_____

_____

_____

_____

_____

_____

_____

_____

_____

_____

_____

_____

_____

2.) How can you let your light shine to be an example to others around you?

Matthew 5:16 – Let your light shine before men in such a way that they may see your good works, and glorify your Father who is in heaven.

_____

_____

_____

_____

_____

_____

_____

_____

_____

_____

_____

_____

_____

_____

3.) When it comes to your enemies, those who taunt you due to your faith or those who treat you unkindly; it's not easy to not get your feelings hurt and take it personally.

Matthew 5:44, 46 – Love your enemies, and pray for those who persecute you. For if you love only those who love you, what reward have you?

_____

_____

_____

_____

_____

_____

_____

_____

_____

_____

_____

_____

_____

4.) Your friends have the latest in video games and game systems, smart phones, and wear designer clothing. Are these things really important? Do they *really* matter? Where do you put your importance? Those items will one day rot in a landfill, but if you store up your treasures in heaven they are for eternity.

Matthew 6:19 – 21 – Do not lay up for yourselves treasures upon earth, where moth and rust destroy, and where thieves break in and steal. But lay up for yourselves treasures in heaven where neither moth nor rust destroys, and where thieves do not break in or steal; for where your treasure is, there will your heart be also.

_____

_____

_____

_____

_____

_____

_____

_____

_____

_____

_____

_____

_____

_____

5.) Soon you will be graduating and perhaps you still don't know what you want to do with your life. Many of your friends have chosen colleges and careers they want to study for while you may as yet be undecided.

Often even these friends who seem to have all the answers will change direction before they reach the goal they have set for themselves. Do not fret about what you will do tomorrow or in the near future.

Matthew 6:34 – Do not be anxious for tomorrow, for tomorrow will care for itself. Each day has enough trouble of its own.

_____

_____

_____

_____

_____

_____

_____

_____

_____

_____

_____

_____

_____

_____

6.) How do you treat others? Are you a bully, ignore those you think are 'beneath you', make fun of someone who thinks different from you, talk about someone behind their back, go along with others when they mistreat someone....

Matthew 7:12 – However you want people to treat you, so treat them.

_____

_____

_____

_____

_____

_____

_____

_____

_____

_____

_____

_____

_____

_____

7.) When you are weak and are tempted to turn your back on what you have been taught, do not be tempted to fall in with the crowd and make a bad decision, remember...

Matthew 10:22 – It is the one who has endured to the end who will be saved.

_____

_____

_____

_____

_____

_____

_____

_____

_____

_____

_____

_____

_____

8.) Do not ever feel you are of no consequence, for God knows the very numbers of the hairs on your head.

Matthew 10:30 – The very hairs of your head are all numbered.

_____

_____

_____

_____

_____

_____

_____

_____

_____

_____

_____

_____

_____

9.) As far as gossip, saying hurtful things to others, cursing, backtalk to your parents, showing disrespect...

Matthew 15:11 – Not what enters into the mouth defiles the man, but what proceeds out of the mouth, this defiles the man.

Matthew 15:18 – But the things that proceed out of the mouth come from the heart, and those defile the man.

_____

_____

_____

_____

_____

_____

_____

_____

_____

_____

_____

_____

_____

_____

_____

10.) Have you ever been on lunch break eating your lunch and saw someone who had nothing to eat because they couldn't afford lunch?

In *Mark 3:11* John the Baptist told those questioning him as to what they were to do, *"Let the man who has two tunics share with him who has none; and let him who has food do likewise."*

_____

_____

_____

_____

_____

_____

_____

_____

_____

_____

_____

_____

_____

_____

11.) Do you have a hard time forgiving someone who has wronged you? Do you want someone you may have hurt to forgive you or hold it against you?

The person who wronged you may not even be sorry for their actions or admit to doing wrong let alone asked for your forgiveness; but what are you commanded to do?

Mark 11: 25 – When you pray forgive if you have anything against anyone; so that your Father also who is in heaven may forgive you your transgressions.

_____

_____

_____

_____

_____

_____

_____

_____

_____

_____

_____

_____

_____

_____

_____

_____

12.) *Mark 12: 30 – 31 – You shall love the Lord your God with all your heart, and with all your soul, and with all your mind, and with all your strength. You shall love your neighbor as yourself. There is no other commandment greater than these.*

If you wish to follow these commandments what must

you do?

_____

_____

_____

_____

_____

_____

_____

_____

_____

_____

_____

13.) You go to church, read the Bible, and have learned the word and know what you should do; *but* sometimes it's easier to do 'what you want to do,' after all you're young, you have time to work on being a "good Christian" when you're older or you'll do better another day.

Mark 13: 31 – 33 – Heaven and earth will pass away, but My words will not pass away. But of that day or hour no one knows, not even the angels in heaven, nor the Son, but the Father alone. Take heed, keep on the alert, for you do not know when the appointed time is.

_____

_____

_____

_____

_____

_____

_____

_____

_____

_____

_____

_____

_____

14.) *Luke 6:35 – Love your enemies, and do good.*

That's not always an easy task; but the reward for doing so is great.

_____

_____

_____

_____

_____

_____

_____

_____

_____

_____

_____

15.) Judging others, it's an easy trap to fall into. It's easy to pick someone's faults or actions apart overlooking our own.

Luke 6:37 – Do not judge and you will not be judged; and do not condemn, and you will not be condemned, pardon, and you will be pardoned.

_____

_____

_____

_____

_____

_____

_____

_____

_____

_____

_____

_____

16.) *Luke 6:41 - 42 – Why do you look at the speck that is in your brother's eye but do not notice the log that is in your own eye? Or how can you say to your brother, 'Brother, let me take out the speck that is in your eye,' when you yourself do not see the log that is in your own eye?*

Are you guilty of this? Of course you are, as most of us are. When you catch yourself doing so just visualize that big old log sticking out of your eye and not only will you probably catch yourself laughing at such a preposterous picture in your mind, but it will make you stop and think before you speak.

_____

_____

_____

_____

_____

_____

_____

_____

_____

_____

_____

_____

_____

17.) Do not think that perhaps by cheating on a test and your teacher didn't catch you or lying or deceiving your parents in someway that was not revealed that those acts are things you have "gotten away" with. Did you do something that someone else got blamed for, and kept quiet letting them take the blame?

Luke 8:17 – For nothing is hidden that shall not become evident, nor anything secret that shall not be known and come to light.

Luke 12:2 – There is nothing covered up that will not be revealed, and hidden that will not be known. Whatever you have said in the dark shall be heard in the light, and what you have whispered in the inner rooms shall be proclaimed upon the housetops.

_____

_____

_____

_____

_____

_____

_____

_____

_____

_____

_____

_____

_____

18.) Invite your friends to go to church with you, be a shining light and an example in your daily life so those who are watching you will wonder at what makes you different. You never know by your actions or in speaking to them how you may change their lives. Perhaps by your example or your invitation you may save a sinner.

Luke 15:10 – There is joy in the presence of the angels of God over one sinner who repents.

_____

_____

_____

_____

_____

_____

_____

_____

_____

_____

_____

_____

_____

_____

19.) Do not be swept up into false teachings. You know that it is only through Jesus that you will receive the gift of everlasting life.

John14:6 – Jesus said, "I am the way, and the truth, and the life; no one comes to the Father but through Me.

_____

_____

_____

_____

_____

_____

_____

_____

_____

_____

_____

_____

_____

_____

20.) You will be persecuted due to your faith and holy life style. Know that Jesus too suffered, can we ask any less of ourselves? Jesus knows what is was to be hated, and you too will at times experience hatred or ridicule due to your faith.

John 15:18 – 19 – If the world hates you, you know that it has hated Me before it hated you. If you were of the world the world would love its own, but because you are not of the world but I chose you out of the world, therefore the world hates you.

John 15:20 - "If they persecuted Me, they will also persecute you."

_____

_____

_____

_____

_____

_____

_____

_____

_____

_____

_____

_____

_____

21.) Life isn't always easy and there will be times you will be faced with things that seem too much to bear. When we think how unfair it us for us, think of what Jesus suffered and what He went through and overcame for us.

John 16:33 – In the world you have tribulation, but take courage, I have overcome the world.

_____

_____

_____

_____

_____

_____

_____

_____

_____

_____

_____

_____

_____

_____

_____

22.) If you have classes where your teacher says that the Bible and the stories in it are nothing more than a fairy tale you can explain this scripture. (Don't expect your teacher to accept it and thank you for enlightening him/her. At the same time do not let him/her ridicule your beliefs.)

Acts 5:38-39 – If this plan or action be of men, it will be overthrown, but if it is of God, you will not be able to overthrow them; or else you may even be found fighting against God.

_____

_____

_____

_____

_____

_____

_____

_____

_____

_____

_____

_____

_____

23.) Do you worry about your past sins and wonder how you can ever be forgiven?

In *Acts 23:1* – Paul in front of the Council said, *"Brethren, I have lived my life with a perfectly good conscience before God up to this day."*

This is the same man who previously persecuted the Christians to the death, binding and putting both men and women into prison and sought those who were believers to be punished and imprisoned. One day he was blinded by the Lord who asked him why he was persecuting Him. And at that time Saul was baptized and had his sins washed away and afterward became a witness to the Lord.

If the Lord could forgive him, do you not think your sins too can be forgiven?

Acts 22: 3 – 16. The story of Saul's conversion.

Acts 24: 16 Maintain always a blameless conscience both before God and before men.

_____

_____

_____

_____

_____

_____

_____

_____

24.) Do you find yourself judging others, when you too are doing the same?

Romans 2:3 – And do you suppose this, when you pass judgment upon those who practice such things and do the same yourself, that you will escape the judgment of God?

_____

_____

_____

_____

_____

_____

_____

_____

_____

_____

_____

_____

_____

_____

_____

25.) Do not be too proud to admit when you have done wrong, but be repentant.

Romans 2: 5 – 6, 9 - 10 – Because of your stubbornness and unrepentant heart you are storing up wrath for yourself in the day of wrath and revelation of the righteous judgment of God, who will render to every man according to his deeds. There will be tribulation and distress for every soul of man who does evil, but glory and honor and peace to every man who does good.

_____

_____

_____

_____

_____

_____

_____

_____

_____

_____

_____

_____

_____

26.) *Romans 12: 17 – Never pay back evil for evil to anyone.*

Sometimes that's exactly what you feel like doing when you've been wronged, retaliating in kind or speaking unkindly about the person who was unkind to you. They will answer to God one day for their actions, as we all will, so keep yourself blameless.

_____

_____

_____

_____

_____

_____

_____

_____

_____

_____

_____

_____

_____

_____

27.) *Romans 14:12 – Each one of us shall give account of himself to God.*

Keep this in mind before acting or speaking.

_____

_____

_____

_____

_____

_____

_____

_____

_____

_____

_____

_____

_____

28.) Don't be led astray and toy with drinking and drugs and harmful things.

I Corinthians 3:16 – Do you not know that you are a temple of God, and that the spirit of God dwells in you?

_____

_____

_____

_____

_____

_____

_____

_____

_____

_____

_____

_____

_____

_____

29.) Don't worry about what others are doing wrong and how they seem to get away with it. Make sure your own actions are ones that will be pleasing to the Lord.

I Corinthians 4:5 – Do not go on passing judgment before the time, but wait until the Lord comes who will both bring to light the things hidden in the darkness and disclose the motives of men's hearts; and then each man's praise will come to him from God.

_____

_____

_____

_____

_____

_____

_____

_____

_____

_____

_____

_____

_____

_____

30.) Do you have a friend or group of friends your parents have warned you against, thinking it best you not hang out with them? You may not see it now, but your parents are looking out for your best interests.

Once you step back from the situation and look at it clearly perhaps you will see why they feel the way they do and want only what is best for you. The choices you make today can have a large impact on your future.

I Corinthians 15:33 – Do not be deceived. Bad company corrupts good morals.

_____

_____

_____

_____

_____

_____

_____

_____

_____

_____

_____

_____

_____

31.) Do you have a friend who is having problems of some sort and needs someone to listen and be an understanding friend? Do you see someone who is in need that you can help in someway? What role can you fulfill with helping someone with their burdens?

Galatians 6:2 – Bear one anothers' burdens.

_____

_____

_____

_____

_____

_____

_____

_____

_____

_____

_____

_____

_____

_____

32.) Do you have an issue with anger? Impatience? With friends or family? Put the scripture below in your room where you will see it and be sure before you go to bed you have cleared up any misunderstanding or forgiven whoever you were angry with and asked for their forgiveness.

Ephesians 4:26 – Do not let the sun go down on your anger.

_____

_____

_____

_____

_____

_____

_____

_____

_____

_____

_____

_____

_____

_____

33.) Just because your friends may use words that are unbecoming or curse, don't fall into the trap of doing as they do.

Ephesians 4:29 – Let no unwholesome word proceed from your mouth, but only such a word as is good for edification according to the need of the moment, that it may give grace to those who hear.

_____

_____

_____

_____

_____

_____

_____

_____

_____

_____

_____

_____

_____

34.) If you think of how God has forgiven you, it will make it much easier to forgive someone else. After all, you want God to forgive you and He asks the same of you towards others.

Ephesians 4:31 – 32 – Let all bitterness and wrath and anger and clamor and slander be put away from you along with all malice. Be kind to one another, tender-hearted, forgiving each other, just as God in Christ also has forgiven you.

_____

_____

_____

_____

_____

_____

_____

_____

_____

_____

_____

_____

_____

2

Daily Bible Reading

Make a habit of reading your Bible daily.

You may choose to read a verse you may have highlighted in your Bible that has special meaning to you to apply towards your life or begin reading one of the books of the Bible.

Whichever you choose, each day write the verse or book, chapter, and verses you read and write any comments or thoughts you have about what you read.

Keep track of your reading and thoughts on what you read for the next week.

Date: _____

I read: _____

My thoughts: _____

_____

_____

_____

_____

_____

_____

_____

_____

_____

_____

_____

_____

_____

_____

_____

Date: _____

I read: _____

My thoughts: _____

_____

_____

_____

_____

_____

_____

_____

_____

_____

_____

_____

_____

_____

_____

_____

_____

Date: _____

I read: _____

My thoughts: _____

_____

_____

_____

_____

_____

_____

_____

_____

_____

_____

_____

_____

_____

_____

_____

Date: _____

I read: _____

My thoughts: _____

_____

_____

_____

_____

_____

_____

_____

_____

_____

_____

_____

_____

_____

_____

_____

Date: _____

I read: _____

My thoughts: _____

_____

_____

_____

_____

_____

_____

_____

_____

_____

_____

_____

_____

_____

_____

_____

Date: _____

I read: _____

My thoughts: _____

_____

_____

_____

_____

_____

_____

_____

_____

_____

_____

_____

_____

_____

_____

_____

_____

_____

Date: _____

I read: _____

My thoughts: _____

_____

_____

_____

_____

_____

_____

_____

_____

_____

_____

_____

_____

_____

_____

_____

_____

3

Learning To Write Christian Fiction

If you are interested in writing, a good place to start is with Christian fiction.

A good place to start in becoming a professional writer is in the Christian magazine market. There are many Christian magazines and church publications that look for uplifting fiction stories to use.

What you need to know:

Characters: In writing a good fiction story you need a main character that is interesting and appealing to the age group of the reader you are writing for. The character should be about the same age or just a little older than the reader.

You will need at least one other character in the story, someone for the character to speak or interact with in order to "give" information to the reader without spelling it out.

One of the other characters may be someone who is leading them astray or trying to, an opponent or opposition.

Setting: The story has to take place somewhere. That doesn't mean you have to say Danielle lives in Orlando, Florida and has a pet alligator in her backyard. If the story is about a pet alligator you can let the reader know where she is by saying, 'It's not unusual to have an alligator in your backyard when you live in Florida, as there is hardly a lake anywhere in the state that you can't see a gator gliding by looking for it's dinner if you look hard enough.'

The setting in your story may take place in a room or in the outdoors where it isn't important for the reader to know exactly where they are. Do give enough of a description that they can picture it as they read. Again, don't say: the walls of her bedroom were pink and she had dolls lined up on her bed. She had a canopy bed.

You can "show" the reader what the room looks like by writing, 'Brianna flopped down on her bed in a funk. She fell across Molly, her American Girl doll that took up residence on her bed. She reached back and pulled the doll out from under her.

She felt like a prisoner in her own room. She didn't know why she was on restrictions. She didn't really do anything her friends couldn't do. Her best friend, Sara even got to wear make-up.

Brianna took Molly and threw her in the corner of her room. She landed by the leg of the white wicker vanity her mother had been so proud to bring her home one day from one of her garage sale jaunts.

Her mother understood Brianna was growing up and felt like she had outgrown the pink walls and canopy bed she had been so proud of when she had turned ten. Well, she wasn't ten anymore and her parents needed to realize that.

Brianna looked over at the vanity and for the first time noticed a few tubes of lipstick her mother had left there. She got up off the bed and took a closer look and found the note from her mom laying next to the lipstick....'

Not only did you get a glimpse of her room, you got a peek at what the conflict in the story was about.

Senses: It's important that your reader feels as though they are a part of the story you are writing. One way to do that is to use the senses. You don't want them to just have sight, but also the sense of smell, taste, and touch whenever possible.

Again, don't say: His mother was cooking bacon. You can make it much more interesting by saying, 'Liam woke up to the smell of bacon assaulting his senses. Most weekends he liked to sleep in, but the aroma of bacon sizzling in the frying pan drew him out to the kitchen where his mother stood over the stove pouring pancake batter into one pan and watching to make sure the bacon didn't burn in another.

Now, this was worth getting up out of bed for Liam thought as he reached to grab a slice of hot, crispy bacon on a plate.

His mother playfully swatted at his hand and said, "Go get dressed. Your breakfast will be on the table by the time you get back."

Dialogue: A good way to get information across is through dialogue. This is where you need to bring in another character or you can always have the main character speak to themselves.

An example of getting information across through dialogue:

"Why haven't I ever seen you before? What kind of father deserts his child and never contacts them or visits them? You certainly can't expect me to care now when you come around all these years later. You're a complete stranger to me."

"That's not the way I wanted it to be. I always wanted to be a part of your life, but..."

"Well, you sure had a funny way of showing it. I'm eighteen now and the last time I saw you was when I was three years old."

"Two years and four months and three days," her father said in a quiet tone. "It's been 5,710 days since I last saw you."

"What?" she asked. "How do you know that?"

"I've missed you terribly every single one of those days."

She sat down hard on the chair behind her. "Then why did you leave?" Tears ran down her cheek as she swiped at them.

"I didn't. I never would have left you. Never. I came home one day from work and you were gone. Your mother took you and ran. I never knew where you were. I spent everything I had trying to find you. Until now, I had no luck."

As he tentatively held out his arms to her she got up and hugged him tight sobbing into his chest.

You can bring about emotion and information through dialogue.

Conflict: Every story needs a conflict and it needs to be solved, one way or another, by the end of the story. It doesn't always have to be a happy ending, but all issues brought up in the story need to be solved.

Requirements: All magazines have a word count that

they stick to. You will need to tell your whole story within the confines of that word count. For instance the word count may run from 1,500 – 1,800 words. Don't be under and don't go over. They have a certain amount of space set up for a fiction story and it has to fit within their guidelines.

Another requirement may be subjects that are acceptable and subjects that are taboo.

To find the requirements for different magazines you may be interested in writing for, it's a good idea to send away for a sample copy of their magazine along with their requirements. Some of these you may be able to find online.

Do your research and see which magazines are suitable for the age you have written for and the subject matter.

Ideas: Where do you get ideas to write about? You can write about issues you and your friends face. They would be up-to-date conflicts people your age face. (Do remember when you write for a magazine that it may be a year before the story is published once it's accepted. Be sure the topic you are writing on will still be relevant at that time.) A good place to get ideas for Christian writing is in scriptures and applying them to the lives of your characters.

Below is a sample of one of the Christian stories I wrote based on scripture that was published in a Christian magazine.

This is for a sample to give you an idea of how to use scripture and incorporate it into a fiction story.

Holly's Reluctant Commitment

by Cheryl Pryor

Holly gathered up her things after church and was trailing behind Tracey her best friend.

"Holly, could I speak to you for a minute?" the pastor's wife called out after Holly.

"Sure, Mrs. Miller," Holly answered, wondering to herself what Mrs. Miller wanted.

"I'll wait outside for you, Holly," Tracey said.

Holly sat on the pew next to Mrs. Miller and nervously fiddled with her Bible.

"Holly, we're one teacher short for Sunday school. I was wondering if you'd consider taking the six to eight year old class for next Sunday."

"But, I've never taught a class before," Holly said panicking.

"You know the Scriptures and your Bible stories. You'll do fine if you'll just be willing to try. I know you can do it, Holly, or I wouldn't have asked," Mrs. Miller continued with a reassuring smile.

By now the church had emptied except for the two of them.

"I wouldn't know where to begin," Holly said.

"The class you'd be teaching will be studying the

story of David and Goliath. Will you try it, Holly?"

Reluctantly, Holly made a commitment.

"It's about time. What took you so long?" Tracey got up from her seat on the steps and brushed her skirt off. "What did Mrs. Miller want?" Tracey asked as they fell into step on their walk home.

The two girls had been best friends since grade school. Their appearance and personalities were like night and day. Holly wore her ink-black hair shoulder length and straight. Tracey had strawberry blond hair worn in a page boy style that came just below her ears. Holly had a quiet, gentle way about her. Tracey was outgoing. Holly lost herself in her art, while Tracey was more into sports.

Holly explained, "She asked me to teach a Sunday school class next week. I couldn't say no."

"Why would you want to say no," Tracey asked?

"Well for one thing, I don't know how to teach." After a moment's hesitation Holly added, "Maybe I'll just call and tell her I changed my mind."

Tracey came to a stop in the road. "I can't believe you would even consider doing that. You never would have learned your Bible so well if someone hadn't been there to teach you."

"You're right. I just don't know how to teach little kids," Holly said.

"Did she tell you what to teach?" Tracey asked.

"The story of David and Goliath," Holly answered. "I know the story well, I just don't know how to teach it."

Tracey opened her Bible to Proverbs 3:26 and read aloud, "'For the Lord shall be thy confidence." She snapped her Bible shut and said, "It's OK to be nervous. We all are the first time we try something new. You'll be a good teacher. With your zeal and love for the Lord those children will be sure to learn. Besides, it's an honor to be asked to teach a Sunday school class."

They walked into Tracey's house. The girls were greeted at the door by Oreo, Tracey's dalmatian. They headed for the kitchen with Oreo at their heels. Tracey began making peanut butter sandwiches. Looking through the cupboards Holly asked, "How about some of these cookies, too? These oatmeal-raisin cookies look good."

"Sure. Pour us a drink, OK?" Tracey licked the remainder of the peanut butter from the knife.

Over lunch the girls resumed their talk. "Do you have any ideas for teaching a class?" Holly asked.

Taking a drink of milk Tracey looked thoughtful. "Don't just read the story to them. You'll lose their interest. I know from babysitting that you have to keep their attention by making it interesting. You need to make the story come alive for them."

"And how do I do that?" Holly asked between bites of her sandwich. She reached under the table and gave

Oreo the last bite of one of her cookies.

"You're making too much of this, you know. You'll do alright," Tracey said as she got up and collected their dishes and put them in the sink.

"I am excited about it. I'm just nervous. I'll pray about it," Holly said.

Every time Tracey called during the next few days Holly was too busy to talk.

"I'll just have to go over to the house and see what she's up to," Tracey said to herself as she hung up the phone.

Holly's mother answered the door. "Go on back to the garage. She's there working on her project."

Tracey stood in amazement as she opened the door to the garage. There stood a life size Goliath that came within inches of the ceiling. "That's fantastic! Whatever gave you the idea?" Tracey exclaimed as she walked around touching and examining the awesome looking Goliath.

Holly smiled as she looked up from her position on the floor. She pushed her shoulder length hair back behind her ears. "I'm just about finished with David."

Tracey peered over Holly's shoulder at the much smaller David.

"I was reading the Bible and came across Romans 12:6. It says 'we have different gifts according to the grace given us.'" Holly sat back and explained. "I thought of my art as a gift I can use to tell a story."

"That's awesome, Holly," Tracey said grinning from ear to ear. "The kids are going to love this. You'll certainly have their attention."

"This is just the beginning," Holly said with enthusiasm. "I wrote out a play acting out the story of David and Goliath. Each child in the class plays a part. I even have costumes." Holly went over to a box and pulled out a few things.

"Here's Goliath's bronze helmet." She set that aside and pulled out a javelin. And here's David's sling and the five smooth stones."

"Holly, you're incredible. A few days ago you were trying to think of an excuse to get out of teaching this class. Now look at all this," Tracey said in amazement as she looked around at all Holly's hard work.

"You said to bring the story to life and that's exactly what I'm going to do," Holly said with a huge smile on her face. "The children will all walk out of that class knowing the story of David and Goliath."

"I just feel sorry for Goliath who's going to get stoned to death with the sling shot," Tracey said as she played with the sling shot. She reached over and picked up one of the smooth stones and smiled. "Well, aren't you clever."

"Yeah, the stones are made out of papier-mâché, so we won't have any accidents. And," Holly paused dramatically knowing she had Tracey's full attention. "I'm using my brother's inflatable punching bag. I covered it with Goliath. When David hits Goliath with the stones I'll let the air out and down goes Goliath."

Tracey clapped her hands. "You deserve a big hand. I can't believe you came up with this idea and put it all into place in less than a week."

Holly said, "I just prayed about it and left it in the Lord's hands. That's when I found the verse in Romans. I knew it was the Lord's way of talking to me and encouraging me."

That Sunday the children left Sunday school excitedly talking about the play. Word got back to Mrs. Miller about what a huge success the class Holly taught had been. After church she found Holly to thank her.

"From what I hear, those children have just relived history. You're a wonderful teacher,Holly. The children will never forget that story."

"Thank you, Mrs. Miller," Holly said.

"I know you had reservations about teaching at first, but I hope you'll consider teaching a class again sometime."

"How about next week?" Holly asked with a smile.

Write your own fiction story.

Choose a scripture and write a Christian based short story. Keep the story between 1,500 – 1,800 words.

Write your story on paper or print it on the computer so you can edit and make any changes necessary along the way.

During the first draft, or writing, just get the story down as it comes into your head and worry about punctuation and spelling corrections or any changes during editing (when you make corrections, changes or modify to fit the correct word count).

If you wish you can use one of the verses below for an idea to base your story on. Any one of them would make a great story starter.

Luke 6: 27 – 28 'Love your enemies, do good to those who hate you, bless those who curse you, pray for those who mistreat you.'

Luke 8: 17 'For nothing is hidden that will not become evident, nor anything secret that will not be known and come to light.'

John 8: 7 '"He who is without sin among you, let him be the first to throw a stone at her."

Acts 24: 16 'I do my best to maintain always a

blameless conscience both before God and before men.'

Romans 12: 18 'If possible, so far as it depends on you, be at peace with all men.'

I Corinthians 15: 33 'Do not be deceived: "Bad company corrupts good morals."'

Ephesians 4: 26 'Do not let the sun go down on your anger.'

Colossians 3: 23 'Whatever you do, do your work heartily, as for the Lord rather than for men.'

Hebrews 13: 16 – 'Do not neglect doing good and sharing; for with such sacrifices God is pleased.'

James 1: 2 – 3 'Consider it all joy when you encounter various trials, knowing that the testing of your faith produces endurance.'

James 4: 17 'Therefore, to one who knows the right thing to do and does not do it, to him it is sin.'

I John 4: 20 'If someone says, "I love God," and hates his brother, he is a liar; for the one who does not love his brother whom he has seen, cannot love God whom he has not seen.'

4

Daily Walk With The Lord

Choose 5 scriptures that are meaningful to you and ones that you use in your daily life to guide you.

1. _____

2. _____

3. _____

4. _____

5. _____

5

Biography

Choose one person from the list below and write a short biography.

You can choose a certain time frame from their life to focus on, an accomplishment in their life they are noted for, or the turning point in their life that made them into who they became.

What do you think may have happened for them to have made the choices they did? Did they pay a price for their choice? Do you think it was worth it to them? Did their trials and tribulations make them stronger?

How did the other people in their life react to their choice? Do you think they may have lost friends over their actions? Gained new friends? Would you describe their choices as worldly or spiritual?

Choose 1 person from the list below or write about a person of your own choice.

1. Martin Luther

2. John Wycliffe

3. Joan of Arc

4. Mother Teresa

5. Billy Sunday

6. Dwight Moody

7. J.R.R. Tolkien

8. C. S. Lewis

9. John Sebastian Bach

10. George Frideric Handel

11. Rembrandt Harmensz Van Rijn

12. Mary, mother of Jesus

13. Joseph, father of Jesus

14. Mary Magdalene

15. One of Jesus' siblings

Or you may write of someone of your own choosing who may have influenced or inspired you.

6

Christian Music

The hymns we sing in church are songs of praise we sing that are not only pleasing to God, but they help us to focus on the Lord, and are meant to edify us. Hymns have been sung since the time of Moses.

Several hymns we are familiar with were written after an event that inspired the writer to write the hymn.

One example of this is 'It Is Well With My Soul.'

Do a little research and discover what occurred that inspired Horatio Spafford to write this moving hymn.

7

My Positive Influence

Who has influenced you in a positive way in your Christian walk?

To influence one is the capacity to have an effect on the character, development, or behavior of someone.

For someone to have a positive influence on you is someone who cares enough to spend the time to encourage or lead you.

Perhaps it is someone you have seen and been inspired by and it is their example that has influenced you and inspired you to strive to be a better person.

Write about the person who has most inspired you and how they have done so.

_____

_____

_____

_____

8

Living A Godly Life

Each day read one of the scriptures below and write how you should apply it to your life.

1.) *Ephesians 6:11 – 13 – Put on the full armor of God that you may be able to stand firm against the schemes of the devil. For our struggle is not against flesh and blood, but against the rulers, against the powers, against the world forces of this darkness, against the spiritual forces in the heavenly places. Therefore, take up the full armor of God that you may be able to resist in the evil day, and having done everything, to stand firm.*

_____

_____

_____

_____

_____

_____

_____

_____

_____

_____

_____

_____

_____

_____

2.) *Phil. 2:3 – 4 – Do nothing from selfishness or empty conceit, but with humility of mind let each of you regard one another as more important than himself; do not merely look out for your own personal interests, but also for the interests of others.*

_____

_____

_____

_____

_____

_____

_____

_____

_____

_____

_____

_____

_____

3.) *Phil. 2: 14 – 15 – Do all things without grumbling or disputing; that you may prove yourselves to be blameless and innocent, children of God above reproach in the midst of a crooked and perverse generation, among whom you appear as lights in the world.*

_____

_____

_____

_____

_____

_____

_____

_____

_____

_____

_____

_____

_____

_____

4.) *Phil 4: 8 – Whatever is true, whatever is honorable, whatever is right, whatever is pure, whatever is lovely, whatever is of good repute, if there is any excellence and if anything worthy of praise, let your mind dwell on these things.*

_____

_____

_____

_____

_____

_____

_____

_____

_____

_____

_____

_____

_____

_____

5.) *Hebrews 6: 10 – God is not unjust as to forget your work and the love which you have shown toward His name.*

_____

_____

_____

_____

_____

_____

_____

_____

_____

_____

_____

_____

_____

6.) *James 4: 17 – To one who knows the right thing to do and does not do it, to him it is sin.*

_____

_____

_____

_____

_____

_____

_____

_____

_____

_____

_____

7.) *I Peter 5: 8 – Be on the alert. Your adversary, the devil, prowls about like a roaring lion, seeking someone to devour.*

_____

_____

_____

_____

_____

_____

_____

_____

_____

_____

_____

_____

_____

_____

_____

8.) *II Peter 1:5 – 10 – Supplying all diligence to your faith, supply moral excellence and in your moral excellence knowledge; and in your knowledge self-control, perserverance, and in your perserverance godliness; and in your godliness brotherly kindness and in your brotherly kindness love. For if these qualities are yours and are increasing, they render you neither useless nor unfruitful in the true knowledge of our Lord Jesus Christ. For he who lacks these qualities is blind or short-sighted having forgotten his purification from his former sins. Be all the more diligent to make certain about His calling and choosing you; for as long as you practice these things, you will never stumble.*

_____

_____

_____

_____

_____

_____

_____

_____

_____

_____

_____

_____

_____

_____

9.) *I John 3:18 'Let us not love with word or tongue, but in deed and truth.'*

_____

_____

_____

_____

_____

_____

_____

_____

_____

_____

_____

10.) *I John 8: 7 – 'He who is without sin among you, let him be the one to throw a stone at her.'*

_____

_____

_____

_____

_____

_____

_____

_____

_____

_____

_____

_____

9

Inspirational Quotes

Quotes that impact us in a positive way are meant to inspire us.

Years before I ever thought of becoming a writer I had a creative writing teacher in high school who at the beginning of the class would write a saying or quote on the blackboard. The only instructions given us were to start writing and turn in our papers at the end of the class. At the time I thought that was the laziest teacher I ever had, yet decades later I still use these writing exercises quite frequently. Whether they are used to incorporate into a story or as a means to make us think they can be a very effective tool in not only our writing but to use in our own lives.
...So, start writing.

On the following pages are 10 inspirational quotes. Each day take one of these quotes and write how it may influence and inspire you or what it means to you.

1.) Life is 10% of what happens to us and 90% how we react to it.

_____

_____

2. When I let go of what I am, I become what I might be.

3. Don't worry about failures, worry about the chances you miss when you don't even try.

_____

_____

_____

_____

_____

_____

_____

_____

_____

4. Stay away from people who try to belittle you. Small people always do that, but the really great makes you feel that, you too, can become great.

_____

_____

_____

_____

_____

_____

_____

_____

_____

_____

5. It is during our darkest moments that we must focus to see the light.

_____

_____

_____

_____

_____

_____

_____

_____

6. Try to be a rainbow in someone's cloud.

_____

_____

_____

_____

_____

_____

_____

_____

_____

7. Don't judge each day by the harvest you reap, but by the seeds you plant.

_____

_____

_____

_____

_____

_____

_____

_____

8. If you want to lift yourself up, lift up someone else.

_____

_____

_____

_____

_____

_____

_____

_____

9. No one can make you feel inferior without your consent.

_____

_____

_____

_____

_____

_____

10. It is far better to be alone, than to be in bad company.

10

What Is Your Viewpoint?

1) One of the arguments on the topic of abortion is the question of when does life begin. What is your opinion on this topic?

_____

_____

_____

_____

_____

_____

_____

_____

_____

2) Is heaven and hell real?

_____

_____

_____

_____

_____

_____

_____

_____

3) There is so much talk about racism these days, do you think it is a person's skin color that matters to Jesus, or what is in their heart?

_____

_____

_____

_____

_____

_____

4) Why is it not OK that after I have accepted Christ as my Savior to just act like I did before? Why must I change?

_____

_____

_____

_____

_____

_____

_____

_____

_____

5) In what way do you feel a Christian should be involved in politics?

_____

_____

_____

_____

_____

_____

_____

_____

_____

_____

6) What is a hero? What qualities or character traits should a person look for in a person they look up to?

_____

_____

_____

_____

_____

_____

_____

_____

_____

11

Journal

Throughout history people were inclined to keep journals. Their journals could have been their daily thoughts, trials , tribulations and triumphs, or it could have been notes on their business life or what was happening in the world at the time.

Start keeping your own daily journal.

Below is a starting point for you to start your journal.

Date: _____

_____

_____

_____

_____

_____

_____

_____

Date: _____

Date: _____

Date: _____

Date: _____

Date: _____

Date: _____

Date: _____

Date: _____

Date: _____

12

Selfless Acts

It pleases the Lord when we do a kind act for others.

Throughout the next few weeks or months pick one of these selfless acts once a day, once a week, or when you feel so inclined to do something nice for someone and write about your experience, how it affected the other person, and how it made you feel.

While you will find that you have made someone else's day a better day; you will also find that you too have been uplifted.

1. Set the table or wash the dishes for your mom without being asked.

_____

_____

_____

_____

_____

_____

_____

_____

_____

_____

2. Reach out to others in a positive way on social media. Be an inspiration and invite three of your friends to do the same. Have each of them encourage three more people to do the same and pass it on. See how quickly the idea grows.

_____

_____

_____

_____

_____

_____

_____

_____

_____

_____

3. Start a teen club for Christians with the purpose of the club being to: encourage one another, help others in need, socialize with like-minded friends...

_____

_____

_____

_____

_____

_____

_____

_____

4. Have a 'No Negativity Day' – a day of no complaints, but only praise and thankfulness.

_____

_____

_____

_____

_____

5. Encourage the teens in your church to bring in canned food to give to a needy family and donate it anonymously. Ask families in the church to donate a $5 - $10 gas card, a gift card from Walmart or other inexpensive store, McDonald's (if the needy family has children), and other gift cards they may find useful.

6. Encourage someone by a kind word or compliment.

_____

_____

_____

_____

_____

_____

_____

_____

7. Have a _'Random Act of Kindness Day'_. Encourage your friends to be involved in doing the same.

_____

_____

_____

_____

_____

_____

_____

_____

_____

8. Tell your dad about one of your favorite memories of time spent with him.

_____

_____

_____

_____

_____

_____

_____

_____

_____

9. Do something nice for your siblings. If it's a younger sibling they may enjoy you spending time playing with them. For an older sibling offer to help them with their chores.

_____

_____

_____

_____

_____

_____

_____

_____

10. If you have a social media page put out a scripture
a day or week for encouragement to those who read it.

_____

_____

_____

_____

_____

_____

_____

_____

_____

11. If you have your driver's license take a grandparent out for a ice cream sundae; if you don't drive, take over the ingredients and make it at their house and spend some fun time with them.

_____

_____

_____

_____

_____

_____

_____

_____

12. Tell someone who has done something nice for you in the past how much that kind act meant to you.

_____

_____

_____

_____

_____

_____

_____

_____

_____

_____

13. Volunteer: It could be at a food bank, you could collect socks or blankets for the homeless, fill shoe boxes with small goodies for Christmas, mow the lawn for an elderly shut in, visit shut ins, volunteer at a children's hospital, help your mother clean house, or something that you come up with on your own...

_____

_____

_____

_____

_____

_____

_____

_____

_____

14. Pick up the phone and call your grandparents and let them know how important they are to you – they will be overwhelmed with joy.

_____

_____

_____

_____

_____

_____

_____

_____

_____

15. Introduce yourself and your friends to someone who is new and may feel uncomfortable in a new situation.

_____

_____

_____

_____

_____

_____

_____

_____

_____

16. Do something using the "gift" God has blessed you with...and before you say you don't have a gift, look deep – you know you do, even if it is just making someone else feel important or to smile at someone...you'll be amazed at the difference you may make in their life.

_____

_____

_____

_____

_____

_____

17. Do a 5K run for a charity and encourage others to join you.

_____

_____

_____

_____

_____

_____

_____

_____

18. Offer to help in a Bible class with young ones.

_____

_____

_____

_____

_____

_____

19. If you have said or done something to hurt someone ask for their forgiveness.

20. Fix a meal (with help if needed) for a family with a new baby, an elderly shut-in, someone who has been in the hospital, or someone struggling financially.

13

For Your Spiritual Growth

1. Read one scripture everyday at the beginning of the day and keep that in mind throughout the day.

_____

_____

_____

_____

_____

2. Take time everyday to pray.

_____

_____

_____

_____

_____

3. What is God's gift to you? How can you use this gift to give to Him in return?

_____

_____

_____

_____

_____

_____

4. Give thanks for a blessing you have received.

_____

_____

_____

_____

_____

5. Pray for the Christians who are persecuted around the world.

_____

_____

_____

_____

_____

_____

6. Keep a list of people you need to pray for and of their specific needs. Pray daily for them.

_____

_____

_____

_____

_____

7. Be able to own it when you are wrong and admit it.

_____

_____

_____

_____

8. Financial responsibility - Are you thrifty or a spendthrift? Do you put money away for another day or burn a hole in your pocket as soon as you have some money? Learn how to be a good steward of your

money.

_____

_____

_____

_____

_____

9. Become a daily Bible reader.

_____

_____

_____

_____

_____

10. We grow in strength and character when we face difficulties; handle them accordingly; these too shall pass. Contemplate on an instance where you had a rough time with something or someone and how you handled it. Did you make the right choices? How did your reaction make you feel, both at the time and later? Would you handle the situation differently today? How so?

14

Debate

As a Christian you will face many instances when you are questioned as to why you believe in something.

Be prepared. Know the answers and how to respond to these situations.

If your school offers a debate class this is a great opportunity to learn how to debate a topic from both sides without arguing, but with giving opposing viewpoints on a topic.

Choose one of the topics below. You can ask a parent or another student to debate the topic with you having them take the opposing viewpoint.

1. Creation vs. evolution

2. Prayer in school

3. Sex before marriage

4. Should sex education, gender identity, and topics of this nature be taught in public school

5. Abortion

I HOPE YOU ENJOYED THIS BOOK.
IF SO, PLEASE DO TAKE A FEW MINUTES TO
LEAVE FEEDBACK AT AMAZON. I WOULD
APPRECIATE IT VERY MUCH.

BOOK 1 OF THE SERIES, WITH WINGS LIKE
EAGLES' - CREATIVE WRITING FOR
CHRISTIAN TEENS IS ALSO AVAILABLE.

THANK YOU AND FEEL FREE TO CONTACT
ME WITH ANY COMMENTS YOU MAY WISH
TO SHARE

ARLINGTONAMELIAPUB@CFL.RR.COM

GOD BLESS,
CHERYL PRYOR

www.ingramcontent.com/pod-product-compliance
Lightning Source LLC
Chambersburg PA
CBHW061957040426
42447CB00010B/1784